PUTTING YOUR CARBON FOOT IN IT!

ALL ABOUT ENVIRONMENTAL MELTDOWN – AND WHAT YOU CAN DO ABOUT IT!

Written by
Paul Mason

Illustrated by
Mike Gordon

WAYLAND

First published in 2010 by Wayland
Copyright © Wayland 2010
Illustrations © Mike Gordon 2010
First published in paperback in 2012

Wayland
338 Euston Road
London NW1 3BH

Wayland Australia
Level 17/207 Kent Street
Sydney NSW 2000

Managing Editor: Debbie Foy
Designer: Sarah Goodwin
Illustrator: Mike Gordon
Digital Colour: Carl Gordon
Consultant: Michael Scott
Proofreader: Katie Dicker

British Library Cataloguing in Publication Data
Mason, Paul, 1967-
    Putting your carbon foot in it: all about environmental
    meltdown and what you can do about it!
    1. Environmental protection - Citizen participation - Juvenile literature.
    2. Global warming - Prevention - Citizen participation - Juvenile literature.
    3. Sustainable living - Juvenile literature.
    363.7'0525-dc22

ISBN: 978 0 7502 6757 1

Printed in China
Wayland is a division of Hachette Children's Books,
an Hachette UK company.

www.hachette.co.uk

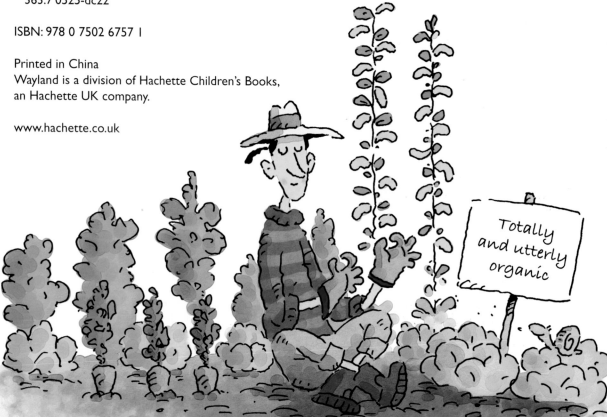

Totally
and utterly
organic

CONTENTS

ENVIRONMENT:
Disaster on your doorstep?

Has extreme weather, or some kind of natural disaster, affected your country recently? An unexpected snowstorm, a terrible bushfire or a severe flood perhaps? Even if these things haven't affected you personally, you're bound to have seen them on TV. They seem to happen more and more frequently every year.

Many parts of the world are experiencing unusual weather-based catastrophes, including hurricanes.

Why is this happening?

Today most scientists agree that the world's weather is changing because of global warming. Global warming is the name given to a rise in the Earth's air temperature. It is thought to be one reason why instances of extreme weather, such as storms, droughts, hurricanes and other natural disasters, are becoming more common.

Global warming is causing other big differences in our planet's natural systems. For example, as the world's temperature rises, ice at the poles and in glaciers melts. It runs down rivers and into the sea, causing sea levels to rise. Many low-lying coastal areas are in danger of being flooded by the ocean. The people who live in these areas may lose their homes.

NUMBER CRUNCHER!

Natural disasters in the world seem to be on the increase:

	1990	2003
Deaths resulting from natural disasters	53,000	83,000
Number of natural disasters	261	337

Most scientists agree that global warming is part of the reason for the increase in disasters such as floods, violent storms, extreme temperatures and wildfires.

Source: International Strategy for Disaster Reduction, 2004

Too many greenhouse gases in the atmosphere mean that our planet is overheating!

What is causing global warming?

Global warming is being caused by a group of gases in the Earth's atmosphere. These gases trap heat, and are essential for life on Earth to continue. If all the heat went straight out into space, we'd quickly freeze to death! Because the gases work a bit like the glass in a greenhouse, they are called greenhouse gases.

However, too many greenhouse gases in the atmosphere mean that too much heat gets trapped. This is what is happening today, and it is causing the temperature on Earth to rise steadily.

Where are the extra gases coming from?

The extra greenhouse gases are mainly caused by humans. There are several different greenhouse gases, but the main one is carbon dioxide, or CO_2. This is released into the atmosphere when fossil fuels (coal, oil and gas) are burned. Most of our energy comes from burning fossil fuels, which means that almost every time humans use energy, they release a few more greenhouse gases.

But the good news is, we can stop global warming. This book shows you how everything you do – how you travel, what you eat and what you wear – affects global warming. And what you can do to stop it...

What happens if global warming continues?

No one is sure exactly what will happen if global warming continues. However, scientists think that the following things *could* happen if the Earth's temperature keeps on rising:

Higher seas levels

Sea levels will rise, causing floods in low-lying areas. Roughly 70 per cent of the world's population lives on coastal plains, and 11 of the world's 15 biggest cities are on the coast or estuaries.

More violent storms

The number of violent storms and hurricanes will increase. Hurricanes can only form when water temperatures reach at least 27°C (80°F) and there is a lot of warm, wet air in the atmosphere. As global temperatures rise, these conditions will become more likely.

Drought and wildfires

Droughts are likely to happen more often. In many areas, it will be harder to find water for drinking or for crops. The dryness will result in more frequent wildfires.

Global warming may cause other problems, too. In the UK, for example, the weather might even get colder because Britain and Ireland are warmed by the Gulf Stream – a current of warm water from the Gulf of Mexico. As temperatures rise, and the polar ice melts, the Gulf Stream could change its course, leaving the UK shivering.

Tackling global warming

There are billions of people in the world – and our population is growing all the time. This makes it easy to think that global warming is being caused by someone else.

But the truth is, we're ALL responsible for global warming. Almost every action we take leaves behind an impression, like a footprint, on the planet. Every time you turn on a light or travel in a car, it results in a bit more CO_2 being released into the atmosphere. Your carbon footprint gets deeper. If we want global warming to end, we must all leave behind shallower carbon footprints!

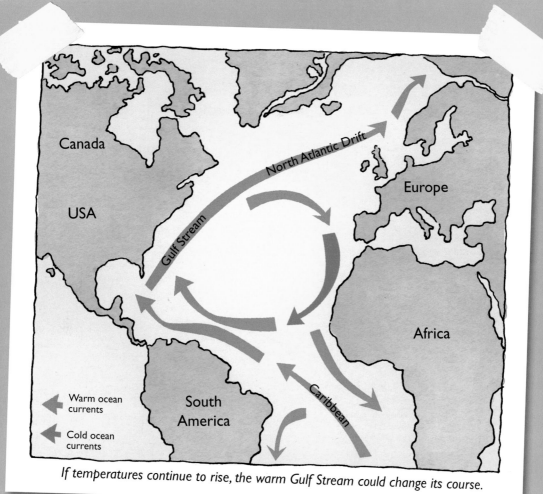

If temperatures continue to rise, the warm Gulf Stream could change its course.

CASE STUDY:
THE MALDIVES

Imagine if the sea flooded your home every two weeks! That's just what happens to people in The Maldives, a group of islands in the Indian Ocean.
Roughly 80 per cent of The Maldives is less than 1 m (3 ft) above sea level. On current predictions, most of the country will be under water in 100 years.

PEOPLE:
Shallow or deep footprints?

We know what causes global warming, and how to stop it. We know that we need to reduce the depth of our carbon footprints, but so far we humans have not been very good at actually doing it! In fact, our carbon footprints just seem to be getting deeper...

Deeper footprints

There are two main reasons why our carbon footprints are getting deeper. The first is to do with the number of people on Earth. The second is to do with the way we live our lives.

Population overload!

The Earth's population is already nearly 7 billion people, and it is steadily rising. Because our population is growing, each of us needs to have a slightly shallower footprint each year, just for our combined, total footprint to stay the same. For things to really improve, we will each need *much* shallower footprints...

Modern lifestyles, such as big cars, big houses and air travel, have a BIG carbon footprint.

Carbon lifestyles

People who live in richer, more developed countries have the deepest carbon footprints. They have homes with heating and air conditioning, TVs, computers and other goods that use up electricity. They travel in petrol-powered cars, and jet off to foreign countries on holiday. Some of their food is even flown in from abroad. These things all use lots of energy, and as a result their carbon footprints get deeper.

In the past, there were more poor people than rich ones. In countries such as India and China, few people could afford the luxuries that the better-off people took for granted. As a result, they had shallower carbon footprints. Today, however, countries like India and China are becoming increasingly wealthy. Their citizens can now afford luxury goods such as foreign cars and TVs, and because of this, their carbon footprints are getting deeper.

NUMBER CRUNCHER!

These figures show the carbon emissions per person in 2006 from seven different countries, plus the percentage change between 1996 and 2006:

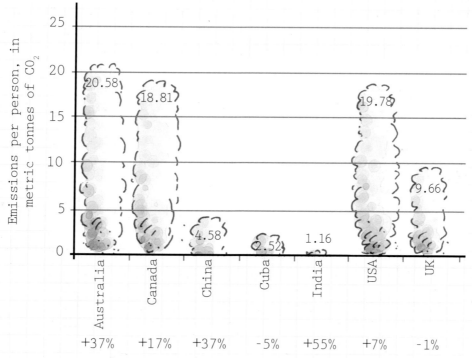

Source: The Guardian, 2009

ENERGY:
Turning up the heat

How many different sources of energy will you use today? Perhaps you'll use gas for cooking, oil for transport or electricity to power your laptop? Energy use is closely linked to our carbon footprints. The more energy we use, the deeper our carbon footprints.

Test yourself!

How many times do you use or recharge electrical gadgets each week? Try keeping a log of how many times a day you use or recharge:

1. A laptop or computer for keeping up with social networking websites

2. An iPod or MP3 player for downloading or listening to music

3. A mobile phone (smartphones are especially power-hungry)

4. Stereo, iPod docking station, TV or DVD player

At the end of the week, count up how long in total you have been 'plugged in'. The longer you've been plugged in, the deeper your carbon footprint!

Where does our energy come from?

Typical sources of energy in wealthy countries are coal, oil, gas and electricity. Each of these is harmful to the environment – even electricity, which many people think is a 'clean' fuel.

Diary of an Eco-Teen

Wednesday 10th

The world is heating up! I MUST save energy. So, from now on, I promise to:

1) Switch off my laptop, TV and DVD at the socket.

2) Wear extra sweaters when it's cold, NOT beg Mum to turn up the heating.

3) Walk to school!

NUMBER CRUNCHER!

Fossil fuels do not all emit the same amount of CO_2 for each unit of electricity they produce. Most of the world's electricity comes from coal-fired power stations.

(These figures do not include the energy cost of building the power station.)

Source: US Environmental Protection Agency

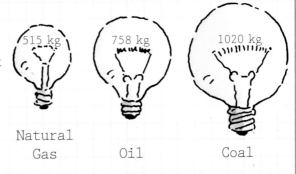

515 kg 758 kg 1020 kg

Natural Gas   Oil   Coal

kg of CO_2/unit of electricity

Electricity

Using electricity does not produce carbon emissions, but most electricity we use is not 'clean'. It is made by burning fossil fuels, usually coal or gas. So, if you travel in an electric car, it's true that the car produces little pollution. But making the electricity that powers the car *did* produce pollution. All that's happened is that the carbon emissions have been hidden, further back in the chain of energy.

Electricity can be produced using far less-polluting energy sources, such as hydro, wind, solar or geothermal power (see pages 12–13). Today, many people want more electricity produced in this way.

Coal, oil and gas

These are called fossil fuels, because they come from the remains of ancient creatures or plants. Most fossil fuels have been buried for millions of years. The carbon they contain has been stored harmlessly over this time, having no effect on the atmosphere. But when fossil fuels are burned, carbon is released into the atmosphere as CO_2 – adding to global warming.

The remains of ancient creatures and plants are buried under the Earth's surface, in the form of fossil fuels.

Are there alternatives to fossil fuels?

Our energy doesn't have to come from fossil fuels – there are plenty of alternatives. And unlike fossil fuels, which will one day run out, some of these energy sources are constantly replaced by natural processes.

Hydroelectricity

The power of flowing water can be harnessed to turn giant turbines, which then generate electricity. Most hydroelectricity comes from water flowing downhill, from specially built lakes and through dams. The movement of waves and tides can also be used to generate electricity.

Geothermal power

Heat deep inside the Earth can be used for heating, hot water and to make electricity. Sometimes, it occurs naturally as steam or hot water. In Iceland and New Zealand, for example, geothermal power is a very important energy source.

Solar power

The sun's energy (which we feel as heat), can be used to heat water in solar panels, or converted into electricity by using special photovoltaic cells. Inside these panels, sunlight triggers a chemical reaction that releases electricity.

There's so much geothermal power locked inside the Earth, it sometimes bursts out! This is an alternative source of energy, which humans can use.

NUMBER CRUNCHER!

Compared to fossil fuels, producing a unit of electricity using renewable energy sources has a much smaller effect on the environment. (These figures do not include the energy cost of building the power station.)

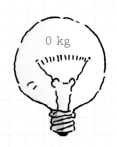
0 kg

0 kg

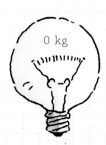
0 kg

Solar, Wind and Geothermal

Hydroelectricity*

Nuclear Power**

kg of CO_2/unit of electricity

* However, decaying vegetation in a new lake behind a hydro dam can cause methane, a greenhouse gas, to be released
** But nuclear power does cause other long-term environmental problems

Source: US Environmental Protection Agency

Wind power

The force of the wind can be used to turn huge propellers, creating electricity. But many people do not want big wind turbines erected near their homes, and there are often protests before wind farms are built.

Nuclear power

Nuclear power can provide huge amounts of electricity with few carbon emissions, but is harmful to the environment in other ways. Nuclear power stations are built using vast quantities of concrete, which is a major source of CO_2. They also produce radioactive waste, which remains toxic for many thousands of years.

At the moment, hydroelectricity is the only alternative to fossil fuels that provides a significant percentage of the world's overall energy use.

Some people don't like the look of wind turbines – but plenty of others think they are a great idea!

Warming wood

In less developed countries, many homes do not have electricity or on-tap energy of any kind. Instead, people use wood for cooking and heating. Since trees store carbon in their structure, burning wood from trees releases carbon into the atmosphere, adding to global warming.

The need for trees

If trees are cut down for fuel or timber, they no longer draw in and store carbon from the atmosphere. But if trees are replanted to replace them, they eventually take in the CO_2 they released. Try to use timber from sustainable sources – where trees are replanted for those cut down.

CASE STUDY:
COOKING WITH SUNLIGHT

Imagine cooking your food in a suitcase! In hot countries such as India and Nepal – where trees have been cut down for fuel – that's just what people have started doing as a way of reducing their carbon footprint. It's a pretty special suitcase, though: it's an insulated metal box lined in black, with a second, inner lid made of glass. In bright sunlight, the box reaches over 100°C (212°F) which is hot enough to cook food. These solar cookers have helped to reduce the number of trees that need to be cut down for fuel.

Trees, global warming and the carbon cycle

Trees and plants provide one of the Earth's vital defences against global warming. They act as storehouses for carbon that would otherwise be in the atmosphere.

Fossil fuels

1. Trees and plants store carbon from the atmosphere
2. Animals eat plants
3. Decaying plants and animals eventually form fossil fuels
4. Burning trees and respiring animals release CO_2
5. Burning fossil fuels releases CO_2
6. Carbon (in the form of CO_2 emissions) increases in the atmosphere

TRAVEL:
Getting from A to B - and avoiding C

Okay, the science bit: C is the chemical symbol for carbon. Many of our individual CO_2 emissions come from travel, especially motor vehicles. So avoiding putting more 'C' into the atmosphere, as you travel from A to B, is a good place to start making your carbon footprint shallower!

Test yourself!

How many different methods of transport do you use in one week? Keep a note of how many journeys you make that involve:

1. A car with one or two passengers

2. A full car

3. Buses or trains

4. A bike or walking

Give yourself three points for less-than-full car journeys, two points for full car journeys, one point for using buses and trains, and zero points for bikes or walking. Add up your points at the end of each week and this will help you to keep track of your travel-based carbon footprint.

Deep tyre tracks - in the car

Cars leave deep tyre tracks on the environment, and are one of the worst ways to travel if you want to prevent global warming. (Private planes are worse – but not many of us get the chance to go to school in one of those.)

Most cars run on petrol or diesel, made from oil. Every kilometre they travel, more CO_2 is chuffed out into the atmosphere. In some cities in the world, cars release so much CO_2 (from burning fuel in the engine) that it helps to make 'smog', an artificial fog of pollution.

Many cars have only one or two people in them. If a car releases 170 g of carbon per kilometre, and there are two people in it, each person's carbon emissions increase by 85 g of carbon for every kilometre they travel. If the car had five people in it, the cost would only be 34 g per km per person.

In terms of your carbon footprint, private planes are not an ideal way to get to school!

Diary of an Eco-Teen

Thursday 11th

Made up a couple of rules for myself today:

1) Only get Dad to drive me to tennis practice if there's no other way to get there. Or if it's raining really hard...

2) Ask Dad to fix my old bike. Then ride it! Am sure this will help save the planet (also help me fit into new skinny jeans?).

Are buses kinder?

Buses have big engines, and stop and start a lot to pick up passengers, so they burn a lot of fuel. If the journey is less than 20 km (12 miles), and you are travelling in a small car with two or more people in it, the car may produce less pollution per person than the bus. If you are travelling in a large car, the bus will almost always produce less pollution.

Shallower tracks - trains

Trains release more CO_2 per kilometre than cars (and buses). But they also carry a lot more people, so they are often less harmful to the environment (that is, as long as they're not empty!).

Holiday travel

Many of us travel long distances to go on holiday – but how should carbon-conscious travellers get there? It's possible to go a long way by bicycle – just ask James Bowthorpe, who in 2009 set a world record by cycling around the world in just 176 days! Most of us, though, prefer to use some sort of powered vehicle – which means more carbon emissions. So, what's the best choice if you want to head off on a long-distance trip of, say, 1,000 km (621 miles) in total? Here are the options:

Option 1 - drive

Small-car emissions, 3 occupants: 42.5 kg CO_2 per person
Large-car emissions, 3 occupants: 85.8 kg CO_2 per person

In carbon-footprint terms, driving is never the best way to get anywhere. Driving long distances releases CO_2 into the air in exactly the same way as driving short distances. But if you have to drive, the least harmful way is in a small, fuel-efficient car with as many passengers as possible.

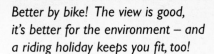

Better by bike! The view is good, it's better for the environment – and a riding holiday keeps you fit, too!

Option 2 – fly

Carbon emissions:
171.0 kg CO$_2$ per person

To stay in the air, jet planes have to burn huge amounts of fuel. This means they release large amounts of CO$_2$ into the atmosphere. But the story doesn't end there. Planes produce pollution high in the sky (obviously!). This is just where it does the most harm, mixing straight in with other greenhouse gases.

Option 3 – train or coach

Carbon emissions, train:
57.7 kg CO$_2$ per person
Carbon emissions, coach:
30.0 kg CO$_2$ per person

These figures show up something that many people find surprising – for long-distance travel, coaches may sometimes be more environmentally friendly than trains.

Diary of an Eco-Teen

Friday 12th
My New Year's resolution this year was not to fly any more, so I'm looking for holidays we can get to by train. Trains are fun to travel on, you really see where you are going, and avoid all the hassle of security at airports. What's amazing is that there are loads of interesting places to go quite near to where I live!

WALK LIGHTLY!

Several airlines offer 'carbon offsetting' schemes as a way of reducing the negative environmental effects of your travel. Money paid into these schemes helps to reduce the amount of greenhouse gases in the air, by supporting projects such as tree-planting schemes or providing solar panels in less developed countries.

FOOD:
The carbon on your plate

What you eat, where your food comes from, how it's grown and how it reaches you has a big impact on your carbon footprint. The good news is that at every step of the way, you can make choices that will reduce the depth of your carbon footprint.

Test yourself!

This quiz will help you work out how the food you eat can affect your carbon footprint. The reasons why will become clear on page 31.

1. Have a look at three items of fresh fruit and vegetables from your fridge. Most fresh food has labels on it telling you where it comes from. Make a note of the different places.

2. Also make a note of whether any of the food is organic, and if so, how many of the food items are organic.

3. Count up how many food items have zero, one, two, or more than two layers of packaging.

4. Add up how many times a week you eat beef, lamb, pork or chicken.

Food's carbon cost

How your food is grown is the first thing about it that affects your carbon footprint. A lot of food is grown using chemical fertilizers. These are added to the soil to help plants grow more quickly, which means more food can be produced.

The fertilizer effect

Fertilizers take a lot of energy to produce. When used they cause nitrous oxide and methane (both significant greenhouse gases) to be released. Fertilizers are washed from fields into rivers by rainfall. There, they cause water weeds to grow very quickly, taking over the river. When the plants die, they give off methane.

Why do we use fertilizers in farming?

There are three main reasons why fertilizers are used for growing food:

1. Demand for food

In the last 50 years or so, the world's population has more than doubled in size. And all those extra people have to be fed! Fertilizers have allowed the world's farmers to solve this problem, by enabling them to grow more food.

2. Shortage of land

So many people need lots of land to live on, so there is less land on which to grow food. By boosting the amount of food that can be grown on a piece of land, fertilizers have helped to ease this problem.

3. Cost of food

It is possible to grow food more cheaply using fertilizers than it is without them. In wealthy countries, people have become used to finding cheap, plentiful food in the shops and supermarkets, and so farmers keep growing it using fertilizers.

Many lakes and rivers close to farming areas can get clogged up by water weeds, which grow quickly when fertilizers are washed into the water.

Where does your food come from?

In the past, most food was grown near to where it would be eaten. It wasn't possible to transport fresh food long distances, as it would simply rot. Today, refrigeration and quicker transportation methods mean that food is sometimes grown a long way away. And just like personal travel, some forms of food transport are worse for the environment than others.

The carbon cost of transporting food

Pick a lettuce from your fridge. The label should tell you where it came from. The answer will have an important impact on your carbon footprint. There are two key questions to ask about your food. Where has it come from? How did it get here?

Food from far away

Food from overseas is transported by boat or plane. The final stage of its journey to the shops is by truck. As it is expensive to transport food by air, it is usually only fresh food that travels this way. Foods that will not go rotten are transported by boat, which is slower but cheaper. So fresh food from far away usually adds more to your carbon footprint than other kinds.

Food from nearby

Food that comes from nearby is usually transported to the shops by truck. Trucks release a lot of CO_2 and this is not great for the environment. But if the journey is short, this is one of the least environmentally damaging kinds of food.

Some of your food travels a great distance and crosses a lot of borders before it reaches your plate!

Seasonal food

Seasonal food is food that naturally grows only at a particular time of year. Where you live, maybe tomatoes grow naturally during the summer time? Because tomatoes grow near to where they are eaten in summer, they add little to your carbon footprint. Eating food out-of-season (for example, tomatoes in February) makes your carbon footprint a lot deeper. Here's why:

● Out-of-season food is usually grown somewhere where it *is* in season, usually overseas, so lots of CO_2 emissions are caused by transporting the food.

● Otherwise, food may be grown in an artificial environment, such as a heated greenhouse, which makes the plants think it's summer! Providing this heat uses up energy, which causes extra CO_2 emissions.

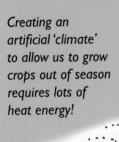

Creating an artificial 'climate' to allow us to grow crops out of season requires lots of heat energy!

NUMBER CRUNCHER!

If you take an average shopping basket in a British supermarket that contains 20 fresh food items, the foods will have travelled a total of over 160,000 km (99,420 miles)!

WALK LIGHTLY!

Your food-based carbon footprint will be shallower if you don't waste food. Use leftovers in other meals (even if it's for the dog!), and remember that many vegetables and fruits will stay fresh for a long time if they are kept in a cool, dark place such as a fridge.

Planet organic!

The organic food movement began as a result of problems in the modern food industry. Organic food is grown without artificial fertilizers or other chemical processes. Since the 1990s, organic food has been increasingly popular.

The benefits?

Organic food and farming are said to have several benefits:

• Many organic food supporters prefer their food to be grown nearby. This means it has to be transported only a short distance, and has a shallower carbon footprint.

• Non-organic farming usually removes carbon from the soil, whereas organic farming retains carbon in the soil. And if it's in the soil, it's not in the atmosphere!

• Organic food, grown without fertilizers or other chemicals, is said to have health benefits.

✳ Diary of an Eco-Teen

Saturday 13th

Note to self: Foods grown above ground (like lettuce) are affected far more by chemicals than foods grown under ground (like potatoes). So, the above-ground crops need to be top of my organic shopping list!

Organic farmers often feel a lot of pride in the crops they grow.

Totally and utterly organic

Shop organic!

Today, there are three main ways of obtaining organic food:

Farmers' markets

Farmers' markets sell local foods. You can often find out where and how it was grown, so this is a good place to buy organic food.

Delivery-box schemes

Some schemes deliver straight from the farm to your door. Others gather together organic food from different places. This means it might have travelled a long way, causing carbon emissions.

Supermarkets

Supermarkets buy food where it is cheapest. An organic lettuce, for example, may have travelled many thousands of kilometres. Organic supermarket food may come with a high carbon cost because of the distance it has travelled.

Air-freighted organic produce may have a deeper carbon footprint than homegrown produce.

Organic = good?

In environmental terms, organic farming has several benefits. Firstly, it is less harmful to the local environment, and better at preserving local ecosystems. Organic farming also uses less energy and produces less waste than non-organic. Added to this, organic farms retain more carbon in the soil than non-organic ones. A US study claimed that organic farming is one of the best ways of fighting global warming.

But organic has a downside. Organic fields produce much less food per hectare than fields using chemical fertilizers. If we only grew organic food, it would be difficult to feed everyone in the world.

NUMBER CRUNCHER!

A 2008 study by the Rodale Institute in the US, found that if organic farming took place on all of the world's 1.4 billion hectares (3.5 billion acres) of cropland, 40 per cent of the world's carbon emissions could be absorbed into the soil.

Packaging and the environment

How long do you spend unwrapping your food before you eat it? Some food comes wrapped in layer upon layer of paper, plastic and cardboard! How much packaging the products you buy have, and what you do with the packaging, have a big effect on your carbon footprint.

The more packaging your food has, the bigger its carbon footprint. And the more annoying it is to unwrap!

What is food packaging made of?

Most food packaging comes from one of three sources:

● Paper-based packaging, including cardboard. Paper and cardboard are made from trees. Trees take CO_2 out of the air, so doing anything that causes them to be cut down deepens your carbon footprint.

● Plastic-based packaging, including cellophane. These are made from petroleum oil, and making and disposing of plastics releases greenhouse gases. The more plastic-based packaging you use, the deeper your carbon footprint will be. To discourage people from using plastic packaging, some countries have introduced taxes, such as charging for plastic bags.

● Metal-based packaging, such as cans and tinfoil. Mining the metal and producing metal packaging causes greenhouse gas emissions, so many countries are trying to discourage its use.

WALK LIGHTLY!

Bring your shopping home in your own bag, instead of a plastic one. If you use a cloth bag, use one made of hemp rather than cotton – it's better for the environment.

What can we do about packaging?

The best way to make your packaging footprint shallower is to use less of it! Of course, some products need to be wrapped in some way, and others are just not available without packaging. So, what should you do with it?

Reuse it

Reusing packaging instead of throwing it away makes it less environmentally harmful. Some shops now give you the chance to refill and re-use bottles and containers, instead of buying new ones.

Recycle it

If you simply cannot avoid packaging, make sure you recycle it so that it can be made into new products.

Diary of an Eco-Teen

Sunday 14th

The world is drowning in packaging!

Just compare this:

1) A shop-bought lasagna: plastic bag, cardboard cover with pretty picture of dish, tinfoil carton and cardboard lid.

2) Home-made lasagna: plastic bag for meat from butcher's, two paper bags for vegetables, all brought home in recyclable shopping bag.

Conclusion: there's WAY less packaging when you make things yourself!

Recycling packaging is becoming more common. Your cosy fleece may even be made from recycled plastic bottles!

FOOD:
Hoofprints, not footprints!

Did you know that giving up meat is the best way to reduce your food-based carbon footprint? But what's the connection between meat and your carbon footprint?

Greenhouse gases and animal farming

Every bite you take of a juicy beef burger adds to your carbon footprint. In 2006, the United Nations calculated that livestock is responsible for 18 per cent of all greenhouse gas emissions. And the biggest offenders are the biggest animals – cattle!

● Growing cattle feed, producing meat and dairy products, transport, and clearing land for farming is responsible for 9 per cent of CO_2 emissions.

● Livestock (mainly cattle) emit – through burping and passing wind – roughly 30 per cent of all methane emissions. In global warming terms, methane is over 20 times as powerful as CO_2!

When burping or passing wind, cows give off a surprising amount of methane – one of the most damaging greenhouse gases.

Fewer trees means a greater chance of global warming increasing.

Loss of rainforest

Beef is a valuable crop, and around the world forests are being cleared to help with its production. In 1995, in Brazil, South America, a rainforest area the size of Belgium was cut or burned down (though not all of it was to make room for cattle farms).

Even when the land is not being cleared to make way for cattle farms, it may still be cleared because of the meat industry. Cleared land may be used to grow grain or soya beans, which are then used to feed cattle. Either way, trees are cut down, and the planet's ability to deal with carbon emissions is lessened.

Diary of an Eco-Teen

Monday 15th

Made a big decision today. After reading an article in the newspaper on meat and our carbon footprint, I have made a promise to myself — no more burgers! Well, okay, I'll eat only one beef burger a month — but it's going to be a good one, really juicy and thick!

The energy in meat

Producing meat requires huge amounts of energy (and other resources, such as water). Just look at this comparison of how much fossil fuel energy is needed to produce one calorie of food energy from two different crops:

● Potatoes: 0.46 calories of fossil-fuel energy produces one calorie of food energy, because most of a potato's energy comes from the sun.

● Beef: 33.3 calories of fossil-fuel energy produces one calorie of food energy.

Since most of our energy comes from burning fossil fuels, to get the same amount of energy from meat as from potatoes, your carbon footprint has to be an incredible 72 times as deep!

If you don't want to stop eating meat, why not have meat-free Mondays?

NUMBER CRUNCHER!

Between 1990 and 2000, almost all countries in South and Central America, sub-Saharan Africa and south-east Asia lost between 0.1 per cent and 2.4 per cent of their forests, to make way for roads, farming or other industries.

What could be better than beef?

Eating beef is an amazingly inefficient way of getting the food energy you need. Someone on a meat-based diet, where the cow eats the grain and the person eats the cow, requires five times as much grain to get the same amount of food energy as someone on a grain-based diet.

Precious farmland

Around the world, meat uses far more land (and water) than most other crops, mainly because of what cattle eat. Cows are generally fed soya or grain meal, which has to be grown on precious farmland. If this grain or soya were used to feed people instead of cows, it would take one-fifth of the amount of land to provide the same amount of food energy.

If we all stopped eating meat it would help to ease the problems caused by the world's shortage of farmland!

It's probably not only the planet that would be pleased if people started to eat less meat!

How deep is your footprint?

Take a look back at your answers to the questions on page 20.

1. Where does your fresh food come from? For each piece that comes from your region, give yourself one point, from your country three points, and from your continent five points. If any came from another continent, you get ten points.

2. If any of your food was organic, halve the score you gave yourself for that piece of food.

3. For items that come wrapped in one layer of packaging give yourself three points. For those with two or more layers, give yourself seven points.

4. How many times in a week did you enjoy eating beef, lamb, pork or chicken? Give yourself two points for each time you ate any meat but beef. On each occasion that you ate beef give yourself a big five points!

The higher your score, the deeper your carbon footprint! Do this for one week each month and use your scores to keep track of whether your carbon footprint is getting deeper or shallower!

AT HOME:
Power, heat and light

On a cold day, how high is the thermostat set in your house? Does your family have the house warm enough to wear just a sweatshirt – or do you need to put on an extra fleece to keep comfortable?*

*HINT: more layers = shallower carbon footprint...

 ## Test yourself!

Here are a few questions that will help you to get an idea of the size of your carbon footprint at home:

1. Look around your house and see how many TVs or music systems are on with no one listening to them.

2. How many appliances are on standby, instead of being turned off?

3. How many rooms in your house have the lights on — with no one in the room? And how many lights have energy-saving bulbs in them?

4. How many baths do you take each week, and how many showers?

The panel on page 35 will help you make sense of your answers.

It is worth looking at your energy consumption at home, as we often use a lot of energy unnecessarily.

Quit hitting the lazy button!

How often do you push the standby button to turn off your TV or games console? Just by turning it off properly and unplugging it instead, you could be making your carbon footprint shallower. On standby, the device is still using up precious electricity!

Among the worst offenders are TVs, DVD players and broadband modems. But desktop computers are even worse, unless they and the monitor are both switched off. Even a computer in 'sleep' mode still draws in a lot of energy!

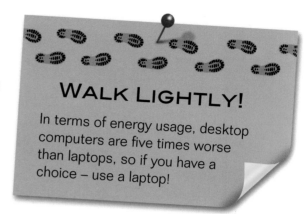

WALK LIGHTLY!

In terms of energy usage, desktop computers are five times worse than laptops, so if you have a choice – use a laptop!

Lighting the dark

Lots of us leave rooms without turning off the lights. We think we're about to come back in – then end up doing something else and leaving the lights on for hours.

Another way to reduce your footprint is to use energy-saving bulbs. These use as little as 20 per cent of the energy of old-fashioned bulbs, and last up to ten times longer. So even though they're more expensive, they still work out cheaper.

Get into the habit of always turning off the lights when you leave a room (unless there's someone else still in it!). It will reduce the depth of your carbon footprint.

Washing - yourself, and your clothes

Our hot water is mostly heated by burning natural gas or by using electricity. When gas is burned it releases CO_2 into the atmosphere, so the more hot water you use, the deeper your carbon footprint.

People use hot water at home mainly for washing themselves and their clothes. Fortunately, there are easy ways to use less hot water, and make your carbon footprint shallower:

Showers, not baths!

Showers generally use less water (and so less energy) than baths, especially if you have a water-saving showerhead. But remember – ten minutes in a power shower can use more water than a bath!

Shallow baths

Some people don't have a shower in their bathroom, or are just desperate for a bath. In this case, shallow baths obviously use less hot water than deep ones.

Only dirty stuff!

Of course, no one wants to be smelly (and certainly no one wants a pongy person next to them in class), but people often wash their clothes sooner than they need to. Before you throw another pair of jeans or a sweatshirt in the washing basket, ask yourself if you could shave a bit off your carbon footprint by wearing it one more time?

Dry clothes outside

Instead of drying your clothes in an energy-hungry dryer or on radiators, hang them outside on a washing line if the weather's warm enough. You'll be using the renewable energy of the sun and wind, instead of fossil fuels – and your clothes will smell fresher, too!

Some people could wash their clothes less often than they think. But do wash them before they start making their own way to the laundry basket!

Heat and cool

One of the ways people use a lot of energy around their homes is through heating or cooling. In areas where the weather is cold, heating counts for half of all the energy used in people's homes. Cutting down on heating or air conditioning will reduce the depth of your footprint. Here's how:

• Make sure your home is well insulated and ventilated to cut energy costs.

• If it's chilly, rather than turning up the heating, put on an extra woolly sweater instead.

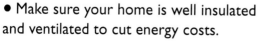

• If it's hot, keep a jug of iced water in the fridge. Half a glass of chilled water will cool you down, and you might decide you don't need the air conditioning on.

When you get indoors, keep that extra layer on! It will mean you don't have to resort to turning up the heating.

How deep is your footprint?

Check your answers to the mini-quiz on page 32. Now that you've read this chapter, the scores below should make sense. They will also help you to measure whether your home's carbon footprint is getting deeper or shallower!

1. Give yourself three points for every TV, music system, etc. you find that has no one listening to it!

2. Give yourself one point for every appliance that's on standby.

3. Give yourself two points for every room with the lights on but no one in there — unless it's an energy-saving bulb, which means you should score one point only.

4. Score five points for a deep bath, three points for a shallow one, and showers are worth two points.

Higher scores equal deeper carbon footprints. Do this test once a week, to get an idea of whether your carbon footprint is getting deeper or shallower.

SHOPPING:
Carbon footprints at the shops

Some people love to hang out in shopping malls and look for new things to buy. Others prefer to browse and shop online. However you shop, your shopping habits (like most other things!) have an impact on your carbon footprint.

Test yourself!

This mini-quiz will help you get a handle on the carbon footprint of your shopping habits:

1. Where do you do most of your shopping: at a big shopping mall, at smaller, local shops or online?

2. Take out your favourite pair of jeans and trainers. Look at the labels and see where they were made.

3. Go through your clothes and see if there are any that a) you haven't worn more than three times, and b) you've never worn.

4. How many of your clothes or other things were second hand, or have been repaired since you got them?

The panel on page 43 will help you make sense of your answers.

Carbon footprint at the shops

Everything we buy has already used up energy, whether through being grown, made, transported or sold. This energy usually comes from fossil fuels, adding to global warming.

The products we buy may also directly affect the world's ability to deal with carbon emissions. For example, products containing wood mean that trees are cut down. Fortunately, there are ways to make your shopping footprint shallower.

NUMBER CRUNCHER!

Since the Industrial Revolution, when the large-scale manufacture of goods began, the amount of CO_2 in the atmosphere has increased by 38 per cent.

Does where I shop affect my carbon footprint?

Yes it does. This is because some buildings are more harmful to the environment than others. Think of the carbon costs of a new mall or out-of-town shopping centre:

● The mall has to be built, using glass, metal, wood and other materials. Making these, and building the mall itself, uses large amounts of energy from fossil fuels.

● The huge space in a shopping mall has to be kept at a comfortable temperature all day, which uses up large amounts of energy.

● Malls are usually brightly lit, even at night, which uses lots of energy.

● Out-of-town shopping centres are often only reachable by car – adding even more to the depth of your carbon footprint.

In comparison, visiting a row of small, local shops will probably add far less to the depth of your footprint.

Think of all the energy that must have been used to build each shiny, new shopping centre.

Is virtual shopping better for the environment?

Internet shopping means you don't physically have to travel to the shops. And as the shops are virtual, they are not built from steel, glass, concrete and other materials. Both these things give you a shallower shopping-based carbon footprint. But internet shopping does have some environmental costs.

- The carbon footprint of producing whatever you're buying is the same whether you buy it online or at a shop.

- Goods still have to be stored somewhere, such as a warehouse. But warehouses can store a lot more goods than shops, and they aren't heated and lit in the same way.

- Delivering the goods to you has a carbon transport cost. But it's likely that they will be delivered with hundreds of other goods on the same journey. One delivery van causes far less carbon emissions than if everyone drove to the shops.

NUMBER CRUNCHER!

The average '100% cotton' T-shirt is really only 73 per cent cotton. The rest is made up of substances, such as chemicals, that have attached to the cotton while it is being turned into a T-shirt.

Internet shopping can be a good way of reducing the depth of your carbon footprint – as long as you don't end up sending nearly everything back!

Which products have a shallower carbon footprint?

You can get a good idea of what kind of carbon footprint a product has by asking questions. What is it made from? How was it made? Where did it come from? For example, imagine the journey an ordinary pair of jeans might have made:

• First, the cotton has to be grown, often using fertilizers. On average, it takes 17 teaspoons of fertilizer to grow enough cotton to produce a T-shirt, let alone a pair of jeans!

• Next, the cotton has to be turned into denim cloth. Energy is used transporting the cotton to the factory, then more energy is used turning it into cloth.

• The cloth is then shipped to another factory to be made into jeans, causing more carbon emissions. The jeans factory may be near the cloth factory – but it could be in another country.

• Finally, the jeans are taken to wherever they can be sold.

Because cotton often comes from poorer, less developed countries, but it is sold in wealthier, more developed ones, its total journey can be thousands of kilometres. It is easy to see why a pair of jeans produced in China, using cotton that was grown in India, probably has a deep carbon footprint.

Check the labels. How far away was your clothing made? Even if it was made nearby, the cloth it was made from may have travelled far!

Fashion – is it a crime?

Everybody likes to look good. One of the reasons people go shopping is to keep up with the latest fashion. But keeping up with the fashion industry might not be very good for your carbon footprint. Why?

Staying on-trend!

Fashions change every season. This is because clothing companies want people to buy more clothes – even though their old ones aren't worn out.

Of course, fashions don't only affect clothes. There are fashions in electronic goods and gadgets, furniture, home decoration, cars, bikes, skateboards – pretty much anything people buy. And if you replace something that isn't worn out – a sweatshirt, maybe – you've taken on the carbon footprint of that new sweatshirt without really needing to.

A passion for fashion?

It's easy to be tempted by the latest fashions as soon as they hit the shops. But will that yellow day-glo body stocking or the sequined hot pants seem such a good idea when you've worn them once? If not, by buying them you have made your carbon footprint deeper without any benefit.

Your hasty purchase of that 'must-have' fashion item may deepen your carbon footprint – but also your embarrassment!

WALK LIGHTLY!

Instead of throwing away your old clothes, donate them to a charity shop. That way, someone else gets a chance to wear them instead of having to buy new, which reduces the depth of their carbon footprint. As a bonus, the charity will also get a little bit of money.

Distressed clothes such as ripped or worn jeans and T-shirts won't last as long. By buying more clothes to replace them, you are just making your carbon footprint deeper!

Distressed, or just plain sad?

Buying clothes to replace ones that aren't worn out is bad enough, but sometimes the clothes we buy are partly worn out from the start! Even if you wanted to keep them for a long time, you couldn't. For example, any cotton fabric (perhaps used to make jeans, sweatshirts or T-shirts) that looks faded or distressed in some way has probably been treated with chemicals to make it look that way. These chemicals damage the fabric, making it weaker and likely to wear out sooner.

CASE STUDY: NEW FROM OLD

Several companies now give their customers the chance to minimise their carbon footprint, by recycling old, worn-out clothes. This idea was pioneered by an outdoor clothing company. To minimise the harm to the environment that the manufacture of clothing causes, the company now takes back old clothes and recycles them into new ones. This means it uses far less resources, and has a shallower environmental footprint.

Can I look good without increasing my carbon footprint?

Yes you can! There are ways to look fashionable without adding masses to your carbon footprint. Here's how:

Adapting old clothes

Just because your clothes aren't bang up-to-date doesn't mean you should discard them. Instead, try altering old clothes to change their cut or style. You could take them to a tailor or try altering them yourself. If you're not confident at sewing, maybe a relative or friend can help? Why not join an online community such as Wardrobe Refashion, whose members give each other tips about altering clothes. The Wardrobe Refashion mantra is 'No buying new!'

Diary of an Eco-Teen

Tuesday 16th

Made up a couple of rules for myself to try and make sure that I:

a) Don't buy clothes I don't need

b) Don't look like a laughing stock!

Rule 1: I Will NOT go into shops just because there's a sale on.

Rule 2: I must NOT buy things the same day as I see them. (If I wake up still thinking I need them the next morning, though, that may be okay...)

Adapting old clothes means you can achieve a unique personal style. Of course, some people's style is more unique than others'...

Buying used or vintage

There are lots of clothes in charity and vintage-clothing stores that have barely been worn. Someone else has already taken on board the carbon footprint involved in making, transporting and selling them. Buying used clothing means that you won't be making your own carbon footprint deeper.

Even if you can't find used clothes that are in the style you want, look for things in a colour and fabric you like. These can be altered so that they're just what you're after.

Vintage clothes don't have to be old-fashioned. In the right hands, they're super-cool. Even Oscar-winning actresses sometimes wear vintage!

How deep is your footprint?

Check back over your answers to the mini-quiz on page 36:

1. Give yourself ten points for every time you shop at a big mall, five for smaller, local shops, and three for online.

2. Give yourself three points for clothes made in your own country, five for those made on the same continent, and ten for clothes made on another continent.

3. Clothes you have worn no more than three times get five points. If you've never worn them, that's ten points.

4. Take off five points for any clothing item that was bought second-hand or has been repaired.

The higher your score, the deeper your clothing carbon footprint!

ECO WHIZZ OR ECO FLOP?

Find out if you are Carbon-tastic or a Carbon dud in this hilarious quiz. Answer the questions as best you can, then tot up your points score to see how you rate against the Eco-Barometer!

1 Your dad wants to buy a new car. What advice do you give him?

a) Get a cool, little city car – with a BIG stereo in it!

b) Buy the largest, fastest, flashiest car you can find, Dad, and put a big, loud exhaust on it. Then drive me to school!

c) Keep the old car. The petrol's probably going to run out before it properly falls apart anyway!

Points: a) 1 b) 0 c) 2

2 Your old bike starts making a creaking, groaning and clicking noise. Oh dear. What do you do?

a) Look on www.parktool.com to see if you can find any information about what the problem is, and how to fix it.

b) Immediately begin a campaign to get a new bike for Christmas. That one's rubbish anyway and never worked properly.

c) Ask your brother if you can borrow his until you can get to the bike shop.

Points: a) 2 b) 0 c) 1

3 Your brother is determined to learn to surf and is keen to go on holiday to Hawaii. Do you:

a) Buy a hula skirt and sunglasses in the hope that your parents will relent and fork out for an expensive family holiday.

b) Accidentally-on-purpose leave the computer on at a website showing brilliant surf in the West Country.

c) Point out that as he swims like a waterlogged sponge, a beach holiday may be safer!

Points: a) 0 b) 2 c) 1

4 What is your idea of a perfect holiday?

a) A train ride to a campsite in the mountains, or next to a beach, where you can cook food from a local farm over the campfire, before sleeping out under canvas.

b) A long-haul flight in Business Class to somewhere hot and far away.

c) A short-haul flight somewhere as hot as possible for less than £100.

Points: a) 2 b) 0 c) 1

5 What happens to your food leftovers?

a) Uncooked stuff goes onto the compost, cooked stuff goes into the dog.

b) Pardon? There are no leftovers in this house – we use everything!

c) It goes in the bin, of course.

Points: a) 1 b) 2 c) 0

6 How many times do you wear clothes before you put them in the wash?

a) Depends on my mood. Sometimes lots of times, sometimes hardly any.

b) As many as it takes for them to get dirty.

c) Once. They're dirty after I've worn them once – even if I can't actually see or smell it. Now, if you'll excuse me I'm just off to wash my hands again…

Points: a) 1 b) 2 c) 0

7 You see the PERFECT pair of lime-green jeans. Even better, they're in the sale…

a) After some thought you buy them. After all, you're saving £20 by buying them in the sale!

b) They're organic cotton… They were made in Portugal… But you realise you don't need a pair of lime-green jeans.

c) You buy three pairs! Lime-green jeans are so on-trend!

Points: a) 1 b) 2 c) 0

YOUR SCORE:

12 points or more: Footprint-tastic! You are an **ECO WHIZZ!**

7–11 points: You could do better, but you could also do worse! At the moment, you are just **ECO AVERAGE.**

6 or less points: Oh dear! You'd better hope they discover new worlds for humans to live on, because this one isn't big enough for lifestyles like yours. Sorry, but you're an **ECO FLOP!**

ECO BAROMETER

ECO WHIZZ!

ECO AVERAGE

ECO FLOP!

GLOSSARY

calorie Unit for showing the amount of energy contained in food. Adult humans need a basic calorie intake of about 2,000 calories a day for women, 2,500 calories for men.

compost Combination of organic things that will rot together. These can then be used as a natural fertilizer for the soil.

ecosystem Group of living things (plants and animals) which depend on each other for survival, plus the environment they live in. For example, a pond, the fish, plants, insects and other organisms that survive there, make up an ecosystem.

fertilizer Substance added to plants to make them grow faster or bigger. There are two kinds of fertilizer: natural fertilizer such as compost, and chemical fertilizer, which has been made in a factory.

fuel-efficient Using the minimum possible amount of fuel. For example, some cars can only travel 25 miles (40 km) or less on one gallon of petrol, but fuel-efficient cars can travel over 50 miles (80 km) per gallon. Because they are burning less fuel, they release less CO_2.

geothermal To do with the heat contained beneath the Earth's surface. It is possible to heat an entire home using a heat-exchange pump, or deep hole in the ground that uses geothermal energy.

glacier Slow-moving mass or river of ice in a river valley, formed by the build up of compacted snow on a mountain.

insulated Barrier to keep in heat or cold. For example, when you put on a sweater you insulate yourself against the cold. Insulating your house well reduces your carbon footprint.

livestock Animals raised for food, such as cattle for meat or dairy, chickens, pigs, and sheep.

offset To balance, counteract or compensate for something.

packaging Wrapping, covering, or containers.

photovoltaic Able to create an electrical current when exposed to sunlight.

poles Extreme northern and southern ends of the Earth. The poles are among the coldest areas in the world, and are covered by ancient ice sheets. Today, these ice sheets are melting fast, which is one of the key effects of global warming.

pollution Harmful contamination, or poisonous waste. For example, when carbon dioxide (CO_2) puffs out of car exhausts it mixes with the clean air, polluting it.

renewable Natural energy sources that are quickly replaced so they are not likely to run out.

resources Useful raw materials. For example, wood, petroleum, coal and gas are all resources.

sub-Saharan South of the Sahara desert.

sustainable Maintain at a steady level without exhausting natural resources or causing ecological damage.

thermostat Device that controls the temperature of a boiler or other heating appliance in a house or other building.

timber Wood used for building or carpentry.

turbines Device with a set of blades, a bit like an aeroplane propeller, which when driven round can generate an electric current. An example is a wind turbine that is used to generate electricity.

ventilated Allowing air to flow freely through. Since the movement of air across our skin carries away heat, well-ventilated buildings are ideal in warmer countries.

vintage Old and stylish. The word can be used to describe stylish, second-hand clothing.

FURTHER INFORMATION

Books

Reduce, Reuse, Recycle: An Easy Household Guide, Nicky Scott (Green Books, 2004)
This excellent little book is crammed with tips on how to reduce your carbon footprint, on subjects ranging from Christmas trees to packed lunches.

Carbon Counter: Calculate Your Carbon Footprint, Mark Lynas (Collins, 2007)
A handy little book that does what it says on the cover: helps you to calculate your carbon footprint. Includes travel, clothes, food energy use and more. There's also a neat little carbon diary, where you can keep a record of your carbon footprint through the course of a year.

The Atlas of Food: Who Eats What, Where And Why, Erik Millstone and Tim Lang (Earthscan, 2008)
This book delves into practically every aspect of the food industry. Although this is an adult title, the graphic information is so clear that younger readers will also get plenty from it.

The Atlas of Climate Change: Mapping The World's Greatest Challenge, Kirstin Dow and Thomas E Downing (Earthscan, 2007)
Winner of an Environment Book of the Year award, this title is an excellent guide to the issues of climate change, which countries are contributing most to the problem, and the nations that are suffering the most as a result.

Internet

There are lots of websites that help you to calculate your carbon footprint, including:
www.carbonfootprint.com
This sophisticated tool allows you to calculate your carbon footprint at home, and for travel, by aeroplane, car, bus or rail. The site also gives you the chance to offset your carbon emissions, and informs on how best to reduce your carbon footprint.

INDEX